Vestigial

Vestigial

Aja Couchois Duncan

Litmus Press, 2021

ISBN: 978-1-933959-49-8

Cover design and typesetting by HR Hegnauer.
Cover art by Kay WalkingStick: *On the Edge*, 1989, acrylic & wax/canvas,
    oil/canvas, 32" x 64" x 3.5". Image used by permission of the artist.
    Photo by Becket Logan, NYC.
Artwork on flaps and interior by Aja Couchois Duncan

Litmus Press is a program of Ether Sea Projects, Inc., a 501(c)(3) non-profit
literature and arts organization. We are dedicated to publishing innovative, cross-
genre, and interdisciplinary work by poets, writers, translators, and artists.

Litmus Press publications are made possible by the New York State Council on
the Arts with support from Governor Andrew Cuomo and the New York State
Legislature. This project is supported in part by an award from the National
Endowment for the Arts. Additional support for Litmus Press comes from
the Leslie Scalapino – O Books Fund, individual members and donors. All
contributions are fully tax-deductible.

Library of Congress Cataloging-in-Publication Data:
Names: Duncan, Aja Couchois, author.
Title: *Vestigial* / Aja Couchois Duncan.
Identifiers: LCCN 2021012502 | ISBN 9781933959498 (trade paperback)
Subjects: LCGFT: Poetry.
Classification: LCC PS3604.U523 V47 2021 | DDC 811/.6--dc23
LC record available at https://lccn.loc.gov/2021012502

Litmus Press
925 Bergen Street, Suite 405
Brooklyn, New York 11238
litmuspress.org

Distributed by Small Press Distribution
1341 Seventh Street
Berkeley, California 94710
spdbooks.org

Printed in Canada

The book is the work of the book. It is the sun, which gives birth
to the sea. It is the sea, which reveals the earth. It is the earth,
which shapes man. Otherwise sun, sea, earth, and man
would be focused light without object, water moving
without coming or going, wealth of sand without presence,
a waiting of flesh and spirit without touch,
having nothing that corresponds to it,
having neither doubles or opposites.

—Edmond Jabès, *The Book of Questions*

In their dream about god's dream, the woman and the man were
inside a great shining egg, singing and dancing and kicking up a fuss
because they were crazy to be born. In god's dream happiness
was stronger than doubt and mystery. So dreaming
god created them with a song.

"I break this egg and the woman is born and the man is born.
And together they will live and die. But they will be born again.
They will be born and die again and be born again.
They will never stop being born, because death is a lie."

—Eduardo Galeano, *Genesis*

In this dream, only women were born.

The men had to be made.

Accretion

It begins millions of years ago with algal mats and bryophytes. Later, when the water recedes, the earth is stitched with gymnosperms, angiosperms, grass fills the open expanse.

It begins the way all beginnings do. Everything is new, unknown, cellular. The sun spills its full splendor across the landscape.

It begins with her opening, almost imperceptibly, toward the light.

It begins with an organism resembling the earthworm. The change is incremental but over time it grows legs, an abdomen, thorax, and head.

It begins with the cambrian explosion, the rapid appearance of animal phyla and the evolution of organisms.

It begins with sight, with the development of the compound eye, a patchwork of eyes or ommatidia, which in their multiplicity provide the ability to see in many directions. There are 25,000 ommatidia in the dragonfly, accommodating its swift flight.

Intersect. It begins with him, the presencing of, a multitude of parts.

Compound eyes can assimilate visual changes at a rapid rate, but such hurried processing has its drawbacks. The brain must interpret a composite of different, high resolution pictures. It must fuse a moving image. The dragonfly cannot differentiate between an enemy and a mate. It must fly very close to the winged other before it knows what happens next—tap, tap, tap—sex or death.

The visual field of humans, of predators, involves large areas of binocular vision. This improves depth perceptions, makes possible the chase.

It begins at night, in the dark interior. She can barely make out his face, but his scent is unmistakable. Pheromones. It begins with this, a lusting for.

Fluttering. Insects travel great distances to satisfy their ecological requirements.

He swims the atlantic, traverses the north american continent, then burrows in.

She remains west, developing in situ, a process of adaptation and random selection. Like darwin's finches, her beak is shaped perfectly to harvest local seeds, her body just small enough to slip between the thorns of the acacia tree.

If she is the product of sympatric speciation, then he is allopatric, vicariant, genetically isolate.

The green hawk moth beats its wings, feeds on the nectar of flowers with the prick of its tongue. From a distance, she mistakes it for a hummingbird.

Convergent evolution explains many things. How different species can develop similar features. How their bodies can fit each other perfectly and yet they share neither chromosome nor tongue. How his scent is absorbed by her vomeronasal organ, signaling something to her hypothalamus that she cannot translate into words.

It begins with his hands, traveling from breasts to thighs, reading the exterior. It begins with her tongue circling his neck, tasting his heredity.

It begins with her arched back, her split abdomen, unleashing waves of pheromones.

He flies toward her cascading scent, tracking her location from miles away by the increasing number of molecules that coat the hair-like olfactory receptors on his antennae.

It begins with lust but mistakes itself for love.

She sleeps with his armpit in her mouth, licks the filamentous muskiness. When he leaves, she wraps her face in the cloth of his shirt, sucking his newly male scent: juice.

Their genetic lines are split by the western cordillera, an immense mountain range dividing the continent as if bone splitting skin. On one side are rivers and valleys and on the other a vast open plain.

At its northern point, the cordillera is cold and dark. Between ice caps and glaciers, the earth hibernates. But even here the temperatures are rising. As the cordillera warms, it wakes and blossoms with an increasing number of fungi species.

The rise in temperature leads to an explosion of insects. Highly mobile, they mate quickly, accelerate their life cycle to match the warming planet.

As the earth warms, her mating cycle speeds up. She goes from proestrus to estrus in a single afternoon. He can sense her swelling labia, the oocyte moved along by cilia down her fallopian tube.

Let's make a baby, he says, laying her down on the linoleum floor. She opens her mouth, her legs, every orifice rising up to meet him. But he has no seminal vesicles, no prostate or vas deferens. When he comes, there is only the sound of it, an echo of gametes fusing.

Convergent evolution cannot explain the biomedical advancements, the rapid transmutation of human systems. It cannot explain what becomes of his secondary sex characteristics, the way a chemical compound enlarged his clitoris and produced a crop of pubescent hair.

Chromosomal pairs generally account for sexual morphology. But there are more options than there are types. It is hormones that determine if he sprouts and she sheds. But it is something else entirely that causes her to gather all the detritus and call it her own.

At its southern point, the cordillera is madre, a high plateau laced with river valleys. Each day they travel south from the volcanic peaks to the cordillera's sloping granite tail. *Here*, he says, *take my hand*. She reaches for it, holds it tightly for as long as she can.

Their journey is striated with extinctions. Most species die out within 10 million years of their first appearance. Hominids have traveled aki for more than 6 million. With each step, the earth beneath them erodes.

Multicellular

Before everything came into being, there was a great deal of waiting for. Waiting for the earth to form, waiting for life to appear.

She waits on her wadikwan, its fragile perch, for him to find her. It takes millennia. When he arrives, he is coated in her musky scent, his body dusted with the damp molecules.

Listen, he says. In the silence she hears the universe.

Four billion years ago, in a galaxy that was not yet named, earth was formed. Explosive and molten, the planet took another billion years to tilt and cool. Eventually it formed a solid crust, cupping water at its surface.

The first life was single cell and microscopic. When the cells recognized themselves in one another, they attached, and in their connection created multicellular species. But such cellular coupling complicates reproduction. Multicellular life requires a germ cell, an egg or sperm, to combine its genetic material. To reproduce.

They are multicellular and yet they cannot procreate. But they are never without this hunger for. With silicone, hand and tongue, he makes complicated gestures toward coupling, toward recreating himself through her.

The first multicellular species were soft, lacking bone or shell. They moved together in small groups searching for food. Multicellularity enabled organisms to exceed the size limits normally imposed by diffusion. Later it permitted increasing complexity through differentiation of numerous cellular lineages within an organism. Creating specialized cell types such as muscle and skin, it rendered the human form.

His adam's apple is thickening and the tips of his nasal bones are beginning to grow. She can no longer read the subtextual plot in the curves of his face. But when he moves, she rises up to meet him, finding something like love in the troposphere between the memory of his body and the person that he is becoming.

Billions of years passed before the first flowering plants appeared. They were late in the evolutionary story, opening skyward long after the first birds pressed their wings into the air.

Look, he says as she watches him unfurling.

Angiosperms are flower and seed producing. Once members of the gymnosperm class, those naked seeds, they appeared suddenly, luring mammals with their lustily garbed fruits. With more than wind and rain at their disposal, angiosperms replicated quickly.

She witnesses his physiological changes, the sexual dimorphism and flowering parts. But the hormones are changing more than his sex. Virilizing and anabolic, testosterone enlarges his organs, forcing his heart to pump more blood. It causes his mind to uncoil like zhiishiigwe, his fangs striking the nearest being in sight.

As he expands, she contracts. Each day, she is increasingly pocked and barren, like a pomegranate flayed and stripped of every seed.

Darwin found such things a problem. The difficult to explain, to describe. Suddenly flowers appeared in the fossil record. *It's an abominable mystery*, Darwin said. Only later would it be possible to trace the evolution of the angiosperm from gymnosperms to seed ferns, the extinct link, and narrate the passage from frond to flower.

Puberty comes late for him; he is already middle age. There is no adolescent body for him to grow into. And yet the hormones behave as if he was fourteen. They excite his libido, kindle his brain.

He is changing so quickly she does not recognize him from one day to the next. One morning he leaves and when he returns, he is compact muscles and dense bones. *Who are you?* she asks. *It is me*, he says. But his voice is deeper and his chest is thatched with fur.

Ecological changes in the phenology and distribution of flora and fauna is not new. But everything has speeded up. What once took thousands of years, can transpire within a few of the earth's orbits around the sun.

She is disoriented by the changes. Some days, the language of it escapes her and she finds herself flying too close to the window, blindly smashing her wings against the glass.

Birds are the only members of the clade, originating with the earliest dinosaurs, to have survived the cretaceous–paleogene extinction event.

Listen, he says, and she rests her head on his newly male chest. *Listen*, he says, *the story goes like this*.

Sixty-six million years ago, an asteroid fell to the earth. The resulting impact was so great that debris filled the sky and blocked the sun. A lingering winter ensued. Three quarters of all plant and animal species died. The birds flew where they could. Those who found sunlight survived.

Many birds still migrate annually, traveling south from their breeding grounds to their winter home. They fly together using cues from the sun and stars, from the earth's magnetic field, from the beating of their four-chambered hearts.

Migration carries high costs in terms of predation and mortality. Birds are hunted, dismembered by power lines, prone to parasites and pathogens at overcrowded resting spots. Migration causes other complications as well. It changes his sex. It alters her dibaajimowin, disperses its narrative arc.

By winter they are housed in the same aviary. Each day sunrise lights the hillside but they are fenced in from all sides. They use their beaks and claws to pick at each other. Soon their flesh is bloodied and their feathers spread like dust around their anisodactyl feet.

Molting. *Whatever comes,* she says and means it. She is good at meaning things. Such arrogant gestures to lash together words and make a voyage of them. To travel the cordillera in the most precarious of vessels. To miscalculate the distance. To tear the map in two.

If only the body could be read as geology, as time and accretion. But it is a temporary architecture. At night, despite the battles, she draws her hands along the angles and planes of his freshly hewn masculinity, running her fingers down his southern tip.

Oops. That is how it starts, a little mistake. Not paying attention.
Or rather too much attention to the wrong thing. The way
his body feels. The way hers feels beneath it. Lust is wanting
another's body to open in ways that it cannot. Splitting her heart
open like a rib. His rib. The one she takes from him.

He is busy sewing things on. Adding parts to the ones too small
for him to cherish. But there is no one to suture her heart, stitch
the mess of it back together.

More than half of all species are insects. Humans are merely a fraction of. He is a small part of her story, and yet he has swallowed almost all of her ikidowinan, the most delicate words.

In a land that is not this land, in a time that is not this time, there is a stand of trees in which lives a bird, or rather two birds but they are fighting and the intensity with which they battle each other makes it appear as if they are one.

In a land that is not this land, in a story that is not this story, there is a stand of trees in which live two birds. The birds fall in love but the feeling is so strange, so unnerving, that they lose their ability to fly. They wait there in the tree for the feeling to pass, for their capacity for flight to return. When it doesn't, they begin to worry and, in their anxiety, to peck at each other. Just to clean each other's feathers, or so they say, but the truth is that it is easier to peck than wait, or worse to say goodbye to the thing for which their bodies have evolved, the hollow bones, the open spaces between them, amidst the crisscrossing trusses, to make them light, to keep them aloft, their entire skeletal system fused into a single ossification. Surely it is not love but agawaatese for which they were intended. If it had been love, they would have lips and the pillowed flesh of palms with which to caress each other. They wouldn't be so expansively winged. They ponder this in the time between the sun rising and setting. So much time waiting on a branch for flight to return, for love, or the passing of it, to be enough.

Divergence

Listen, she says, but there is no one beside her.

Listen, replies the wind as it rattles the dead leaves from the trees.

Beneath the yucatan peninsula spreading out into the waters
of the gulf of mexico is a scar one hundred and ten miles wide.
The chicxulub crater was carved millions of years ago by celestial
impact, then covered by sedimentary rock, by limestone and sea
water, by mangroves and estuaries, by rainforests and grasslands,
by cities and veins of asphalt roads.

Carapace. Collision. Catastrophe.

Look, he says, appearing suddenly out of the ashes. There, in the
cup of his palm, is a thin layer of clay sediment rich in iridium,
one of the rarest elements in the earth's crust, but common to
asteroids.

Look, he says, and licks the dust with his tongue.

As in all cataclysmic events, there were many who perished and a few that survived. The mammalian groups, the placentals and marsupials, evolved divergent traits and claimed a larger range of ecological niches.

She has spread herself too thin, made one too many adaptions until she is unrecognizable to herself. In the epigenetic drift, she is alternating between ancestry and an impossible future tense. *Cherish me*, she says. *Cherish me*, replies the wind.

Placentals birthed fully nourished young and spread across the northern hemisphere while the marsupials and their fetal newborns ranged across the southern landscape. The marsupials reached australia 50 million years ago, shortly after it split off from antarctica. With their tails, they rowed across the terrestrial gap.

In his pouch is another version of himself. He pulls it out and wraps himself in the wet and bloodied fur.

The continental crust has been in the grips of a grand supercontinent cycle since its formation over three and a half billion years ago. Once formed, pangaea began to separate, splitting into two continents, laurasia to the north and gondwana to the south. Eventually it broke into many continental pieces. Even now, in the heart of the red sea, two of aki's tectonic plates are being torn apart.

Rift. What began at night is dismantled in the startling light of day. He breaks away from her as if a shifting fault, the lithosphere thrusting forward until the mantle is severed. But the sound is buried so deeply in the earth, she can barely hear the rupturing.

What's that, she asks. Baswewe tries to unearth itself from so many layers beneath the ground. *What's that*, she whispers.

Scrape, scrape, scrape.

In the dream that is not a dream, she weaves baskets of wiigwaas and fills them with seeds. When the time comes to plant, the seeds are desiccant, their coats split open. Rubbing them together, she creates enough smoke to fill the basket, to fill up the empty space in her heart.

There are four elements that make up 96% of all living matter: carbon, oxygen, hydrogen, and nitrogen. Fire requires just two.

When the conflagration has scorched all of the land around her, her dreams become smaller. The seeds are gone. She has only a small pile of wiigwaas from which to weave a new land to harvest.

Sexual selection and sexual conflict are widespread in insects. There is evidence linking both to increased diversification across the modern insect orders.

Primates demonstrate sexual conflict in a variety of behavioral, anatomical and physiological traits. Because these traits favor the reproductive interests of one sex over the other, counterstrategies evolve that trigger an evolutionary race between the sexes.

Butchery. She finds his finger one morning curled around hers. There in the kitchen with the collard greens. She cuts everything into pieces. A mound of green leaves and red blood. She places the dismembered parts in a basket and hangs it in the juniper hedge. The next morning the birds come. There, in the early morning light, wiikwandiwin, a feasting of.

Female promiscuity among primates has been interpreted as a counterstrategy to male acts of infanticide.

You are mine, he says. And it is true. Every thought, every gesture. But this does not stop her rebellions.

Everything has already been scripted. There are well published protocols. First the diagnosis. Then the hormone therapy. It is a year before his breasts are removed by a surgeon's knife and his torso wrapped in yards of white gauze. Each morning she loosens the bandage and milks him, emptying the drains of blood and fluid. When the gauze is finally removed, his chest is perfectly sculpted. Landscape.

Female resistance in evolutionary biology is framed as antagonistic
co-evolution. After the surgery, she is left with the memory
of what came before it. This makes her an adversary in his
evolutionary story.

He does what he can to erase them, taking the pictures down
and emptying the closets of everything that came before.
The one that I loved cannot be erased, she tells him. *The one that you loved
never existed,* he says.

Primates diverged from other mammals around 85 million years ago. But bipedalism is relatively new. Four million years ago, hominids moved from the trees into the spreading grasslands. Now upright, they could see across great distances, their hands free to transport food and tools.

Ardipithecus ramidus developed differently from her male counterpart. Her subpubic arch was obtuse so that she could walk while bearing the weight of pregnancy. Almost four feet tall, she was shorter and plumper than the man she mated with, but she was the one, with twigs and leaves, who brought the next generation of hominids into the world.

Listen, she says, *there is something else to this story*. In the cave, by newly harnessed fire light, they practiced monogamous pair bonding and it increased their chance of survival.

Listen, he says, *there is something I need to tell you*. She waits but the lie is curled so tightly around his throat that no other words come.

Genetic evidence suggests that homo neanderthalensis mated with homo sapiens about 65,000 years ago. Neanderthalensis was larger, stronger, with a brain that continued to grow into adulthood. But sapien was light and graceful and able to call the birds out of the sky.

In the religion of biology there are descriptions and proscriptions. Often, they are one and the same.

It is not possible to mate across species, he tells her.

Sex is an immutable category, she says.

Binesiwag scream their own version of things from the trees. Amidst the cacophony, neither of them can glean the other's meaning between the raptors' cries.

Evolution is a story whose time span is infinite. When aki rids itself of humans, forest will repossess the cities, binesiwag will reclaim the skies.

But their story is briefer, the telling is only as long as the length of their breath.

Scientists postulate that the thrifty genotype was advantageous for hunter-gathers, especially child-bearing women who could fatten quickly during times of abundance and better survive scarcity. But the same genetic makeup is detrimental to modern humans who have no limits to what they can consume.

The thrifty genotype impacts more than the consumption of food. It causes human beings to drink love in hungry gulps, to try and stave off periods of future drought.

She swallows the milk of it like a starving child, until, finally, inevitably, it dries up. At night she wakes to the sound of her desiccated lips puckering, attempting to drink the dark. There, in the echo of it, is something older, something that crackles in her bones.

The next morning, she wakes in a spool of light, the sun tethering her with its ancient grasp. In the heat of its gaze, she remembers what it was like when he first wrapped himself around her, signaling that coming into the world. Split and whole.

Without him, she has no one to tell the rest of the story. Or so she thinks until she sees the reflection of him, the always imagined him, beside her.

Listen, she says, *those who came before us have something to teach us.* Take, for instance, early homo sapien. There by firelight, the woman threads bone and shell onto a strand of sinew. *Wear this*, the woman says. But she knows that nothing she does can protect him from the bison's horn.

He is silent but she imagines him shuddering.

Picture this, she says. Thousands of years later, near the village of les eyzies in the southwest of france, their skeletons are found. Their necks are laced with abalone and teeth, the bones of their hands almost touching.

Listen, she says, even though she can no longer see his reflection. *Listen*, she says. The woman harvested colored earth, grinding and washing the soil until a red ochre pigment formed from which she painted horses, aurochs, and deer onto the walls of the cave.

But what about the man, she imagines him asking. He would, of course, think there should be a picture of the man.

There are only animals, she says. The man has been gone on a long, long journey. But he is here now. The woman is putting the man's hands deep inside of her. She is the interior onto which he paints his portrait.

Look, she says, *the woman is dipping the man's palms into the dark paint*. There in the firelight, she is pressing his hands against the damp wall of the cave.

For a long time after he left her, she has nightmares in which he is always hovering.

One night in a dream he comes to her with antlers strapped to his head. *I am magnificent,* he tells her. *You're ma'iingan,* she says. There, silently in front of her, he is swathed in fur, wearing the bones of his prey.

She starts whispering the stories she once told him. *Every season,* she murmurs, *they dismantle the mammoth bone hut so they can follow the game.* The woman rolls the deer skin maps and places them in her blouse against her chest. On them she has painted a configuration of anangoog, the fires of the night sky to guide her. One day, she tells the man, these maps will lead me to the end of the earth.

The great apes spawned many genetic lines. From gorilla to chimpanzee to homo habilis who used her unusually long arms to pound stone. When homo erectus found her, habilis was still chimp-like in her demeanor. But that didn't prevent erectus from bedding down with her in the leafy brush. It was only later, when erectus wanted something habilis couldn't provide, that speciation began.

She swears not to say another word until she forgets the naming of him, the making of him. When the words fill up inside of her, she presses down on her stomach, floods her intestines. Her esophagus is stuffed full of them. She opens her mouth and vomits. Every phoneme spills forth.

Vestigial

All vertebrates have a complex network of electrical impulses that enables them to adapt to their environment. The impulses explode like fireworks amidst a sky of cells. Billions and billions of them. And the body responds, a marionette twisting and turning, secreting and digesting, ducking, running, playing dead.

She lies on the bathroom floor for hours, waiting for dawn to come, for god to come, for something to lift her. But there is only the pink lip of sunrise shining through the bathroom window to remind her of what it means to. Bimaadizi, this puckering breath of life.

The endocrine system is an arrangement of glands that affect long-term adaptation. Secreting hormones into the bloodstream, the glands connect to the nervous system through the hypothalamus, a tiny collection of nuclei located just above the brainstem.

Bundled together, they were hunger and thirst, spit and lust. Unraveled, separate, everything became peripheral.

That which begins in one nuclei is often unrecognizable in another. That which began in one time is altered in another.

Oxytocin is the hormone associated with human bonding, with feelings of love. It is an agent in the neuro-anatomy of intimacy and sexual reproduction. During arousal, both the male and female body are flooded with it.

Oxytocin affects human learning through the intensification of particular memories. Every moment of pleasure and injury, of joy and despair, is burned into the soft tissue. When the memory is rekindled by some new event, the conflagration is immediate.

Amidst the flames, it is impossible to see present or future. There is only awasonaago, yesterday's trail of smoke.

After years of fear, fear that he would return, fear that he would not, her adrenal glands spasmed and froze. No longer manufacturing and secreting the hormones necessary for her body to adapt. The caterpillar-shaped glands above her kidneys are caught in their own paroxysm.

Frozen, she lies prostrate and listens for the cracks, mikwam, the glacial dermis.

Trilling

In every family there are genetic pathways, tributaries that guide molecular units of heredity. She hears them calling to her the way dawn calls the sun. She has been asleep so long that their voices have become urgent. They tell her things in a language she does not understand.

Indaanis, my daughter, and then the wind.

When she opens her eyes, the sky is bright, as if she had slept half the day, half of her life.

Indaanis, the ice caps are melting. Watch out for the river. It will flood soon.

As temperatures rise, glaciers and ice caps melt and water flows into the seas. The water warms and expands, raising sea levels. Slowly, the land begins to recede. Soon, she knows, it will be harder to travel across the oceanic expanse.

One night she wakes to an invisible hand shaking her. *Indaanis, there isn't much time.*

The next day she begins scavenging the neighborhood for wood scraps to build a boat. She finds a shed with an assortment of windows and doors but she cannot figure out how to patch these disparate objects into an ark. It takes several weeks to finally amass all of what she needs. She epoxies the stray pieces of lumber together and coats the surface in sealant. While the wood dries, she stitches a flag together. There are no skulls or crossbones on it, just a red heart smashed to smithereens.

At dusk, she climbs into the boat and hoists the flag. There, on the front porch, she waits for the water to find her, to lift her up, to carry her off like the wind.

During the most recent ice age, the seas dropped and the glaciers rose. Now everything is being reversed. Animals follow the water down the mountains into the valleys. They track rivers across state lines.

One day she finds a black bear in her front yard. *Makwa*, she says, *you are hundreds of miles from home.* Slightly shorter than she is, it outweighs her by at least thirty pounds.

When night falls, the bear is still there in the yard, marking the tree with claws and teeth. She brings it a basket of berries and sits on the porch watching through the darkness as the bear devours them. When the bear is done, it climbs the tree and wraps its thick body around the sturdiest branch.

She places a blanket and pillow in the boat and makes a bed of it. She can hear the bear snoring, a husky vibration that lulls her to sleep.

For months she waits for the water, but it does not come. The bear disappears during the day and returns each evening, lumbering at the edge of her yard.

At first, she just brings it berries. Eventually she starts making salads of parsnips, carrots, turnips and anchovies and places them in a bucket that she hangs from the lowest branch of the tree.

One evening the bear is waiting for her on the porch. She hands it the bucket and settles into the boat. The bear moves back into the darkness of the yard to dine on the roots and fish.

Makwa, she says, speaking into the shadows, *when the water comes, I am sailing north toward the arctic, toward ursa minor, little bear, and the north star.*

There are bears there too, she says, but she doesn't mention they are white and twice makwa's size. She doesn't mention the land itself is mostly ice. She knows that as everything warms, the molecules are speeding up causing the ice to shift from a solid to a liquid state. The permafrost is thawing and releasing increasing amounts of methane, further exacerbating polar amplification.

At night she dreams that all the earth's bears are living together on an iceberg. Black bears, brown bears, sloth bears, sun bears, polar bears inhabiting a frozen island in the arctic sea. The polar bears are teaching the others how to hunt for seals and fish in the frigid waters surrounding their floating islet of ice.

When she wakes, she hears the familiar voice. *Indaanis, the temperatures are rising*. Aki can no longer yoke its weather patterns. Soon they will swing wildly between states of drought and flood.

The physiological processes that define life are biochemical reactions, the signaling and flow of chemical energy. Simple chemical reactions increase as temperature increases, but physiological processes proceed more slowly at temperatures above or below their thermal optimum.

These same processes are also water-based. With increasing climate change, all organisms struggle to maintain an appropriate water balance and temperature range for life-sustaining biochemical interactions.

The air becomes so dry she could light it on fire with a match. All of the surrounding creeks dry up and the deer, foxes, and coyotes are forced toward town where the water still miraculously comes out of faucets. She puts buckets of water out for them but the bear scares them off with her restlessness. The boat listing on the porch seems like an absurdity.

Then, one evening, the sky thunders and cracks and water pours from the serrated opening. In the drought, the soil has baked to a hard clay so now water slips across it as if rock. Within days, the town is transformed into a medieval kingdom of hilltop fortresses and moats.

In a land that is not this land, in a time that is not this time, aki spits out its tongue and the spine of a continent bursts forth. Plants evolve from lakeside algae and spread onto land. Insects dine on the green foliage and eventually take flight. Four-footed vertebrates begin their journey out of the water, although some return to reproduce in the dark liquid's protection. Flowering plants spring forth as do bees and ants. Song birds take to the skies. Mammoths swing their long, curved tusks while homo hominids domesticate dogs and hunt the earth's verdant expanse.

In a land that is not this land, in a story that is not this story, she waits in the tree while the water fills her yard, her house, carries away all her possessions. The bear is resting on an adjacent limb, breathing heavily beside her. The boat floats idly nearby.

In a land that is not this land, in a time that is not this time, the woman who came before her, the one who learned to love by firelight, harvests verbena and yellow dock, which she uses to make a paste to coat her pregnant belly. When the man returns to the cave he finds the woman naked, her skin covered in ash and mud. The man is afraid to touch her but the woman guides his hand into the darkest, wettest recesses of her body. When the man withdraws it, his fingers are coated in sticky red blood. The baby is coming, the woman says. And so it does.

When water subsumes the highest branches of the tree, she climbs into the boat with her backpack of provisions and unties the cord. For the first mile the bear swims alongside her. *Makwa,* she says, *come into the boat.* But the bear ignores her. *Makwa,* she says, but the bear is already waving goodbye.

The water is crowded with everything it has swept away. Occasionally she sees the corpses of animals but makwa is no longer in sight. When she reaches the ocean, there are many other boats in the water. She calls out to them, but the chopping waves prevent the passage of any other sound.

Hours pass then darkness comes. Somehow, in the shadows of this violent womb, she sleeps. At dawn the horizon bleeds a pink light. All around her is water, grey and turbid. *Makwa,* she says just to hear the sound of her own voice. *Indaanis,* the wind replies.

The ocean is becoming increasingly acidic due to atmospheric carbon dioxide dissolving into rivers, lakes, and seas. Rising acidification kills coral and depresses the metabolic rate and immune response in marine organisms.

Acidification of the world's oceans has occurred before. Fifty-six million years ago there was a dramatic increase in global temperatures and carbon cycling. These changes caused mass species extinction and the sudden appearance of human progenitors, of primates.

She watches the water as if fishing for something beneath its depths. But it is only a mental exercise. She knows that it is her mind that presents the biggest danger. It must be tamed or it might slip off for hours at a time only to return with a fresh kill in its mouth.

When she grows tired, the voices become louder. *Indaanis*, they say, *the world is only temporary*. In 5 billion years the sun will cool and swell, its diameter expanding to such a degree that it will cast off its outer layers and leave only a stellar remnant behind. The gravity of passing stars will reduce the sun's retinue of planets, some being destroyed, others being ejected into interstellar space. Eventually none of the original orbiting bodies in the solar system will be left. Ishpiming will have no one inside of her.

In the darkest hours of the night, the boat must sail itself. She dreams, and in this way, connects all the disparate parts.

Memengwaa have been used to represent the principle of connection in chaos theory. One beat of its wings and a hurricane loses its eye.

Look, he says, pointing to nucleus. But it is her dream and she threads the sensitive dependencies across the horizon.

You don't understand, she says. *The story of evolution is a love story*. But even as she tells him this, she questions the narrative arc.

When dawn comes, its fragile light startles her. Her own perseverance startles her awake. The boat is still upright. The earth is still spinning. She licks her izinoo'iganininj, holds it up to the wind. It is difficult to make a prediction, but she does what she can. Tacking the sail, she heads into the blustering current of air.

She is not alone. Wiin ombaashi. Lifted be the sky's sweet breath.

Acknowledgment

I want to express my deepest gratitude to all those who made this book possible.

To Stacy Jackson who read and reread this manuscript as I struggled to give it words.

To the one whose love, and then absence of, made the words necessary.

To Renee Gladman who has always encouraged the widest exploration of meaning, making the breadth of this book possible.

To the magazines and online journals who published excerpts of this book: *Tarpaulin Sky Magazine* (as a finalist for their 2015 book award) and *The Brooklyn Rail* (in conversation with Brenda Iijima).

To my friends, family, teachers, ancestors, plant and animal guides.

Miigwech.